EASY PIANO

SIMPLE CLASSICAL PIANO PIECES

EASY PIECES FROM THE MASTERS

ISBN 978-1-5400-4427-3

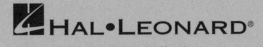

Visit Hal Leonard Online at
www.halleonard.com

Contact us:
Hal Leonard
7777 West Bluemound Road
Milwaukee, WI 53213
Email: info@halleonard.com

In Europe, contact:
Hal Leonard Europe Limited
42 Wigmore Street
Marylebone, London, W1U 2RN
Email: info@halleonardeurope.com

In Australia, contact:
Hal Leonard Australia Pty. Ltd.
4 Lentara Court
Cheltenham, Victoria, 3192 Australia
Email: info@halleonard.com.au

CONTENTS

MINUET IN G MAJOR

BWV Appendix 116

ANONYMOUS

4

MUSETTE IN D MAJOR

BWV Appendix 126

ANONYMOUS

Allegretto

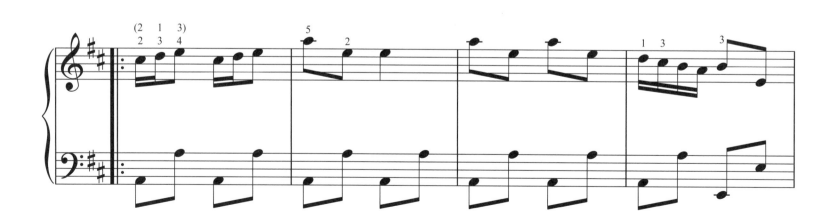

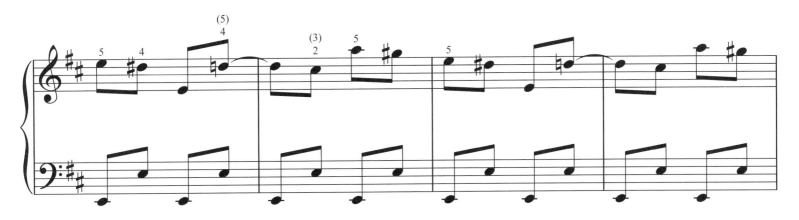

MINUET IN C MINOR
BWV Appendix 121

ANONYMOUS

MINUET IN D MINOR
BWV Appendix 132

ANONYMOUS

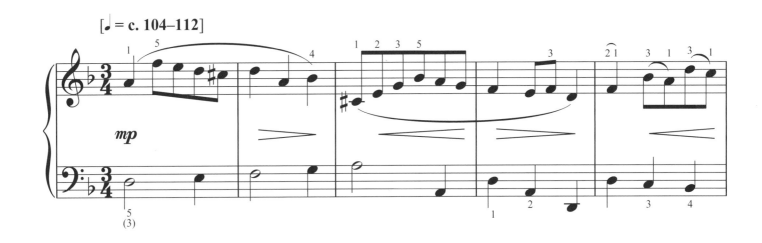

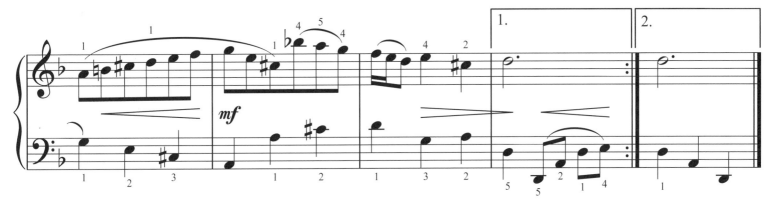

MARCH IN D MAJOR
BWV Appendix 122

CARL PHILIPP EMANUEL BACH
1714–1788

Marcato

PRELUDE IN C MAJOR
from *The Well-Tempered Clavier, Book 1*
BWV 846

JOHANN SEBASTIAN BACH
1685–1750

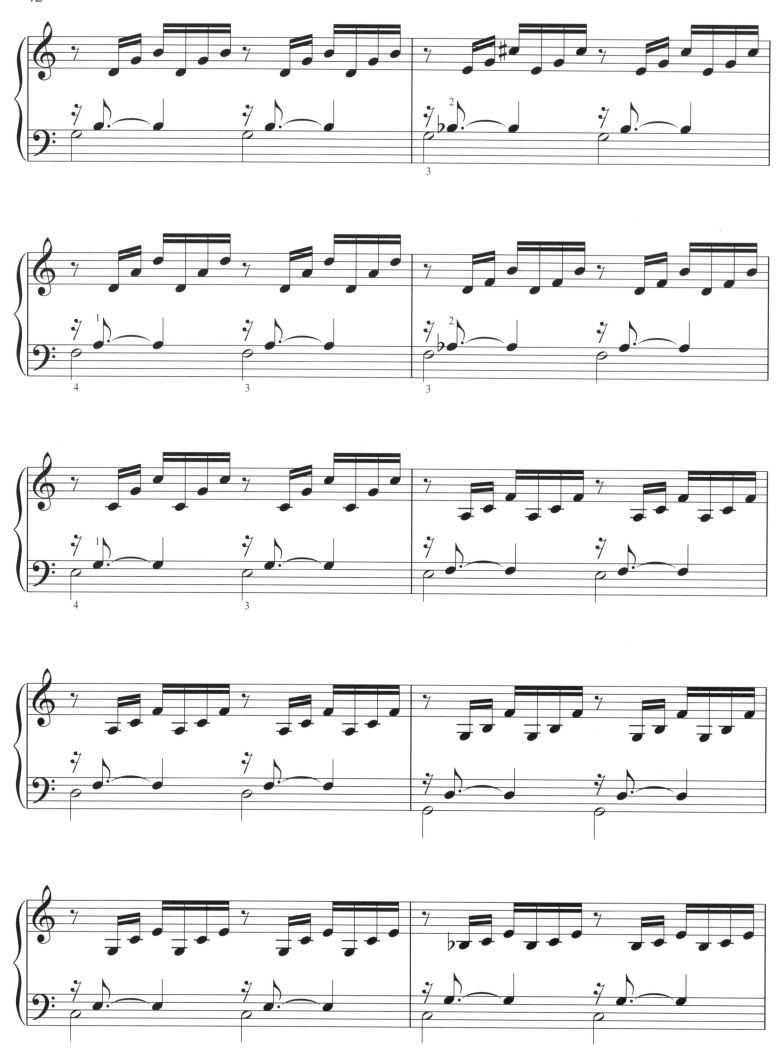

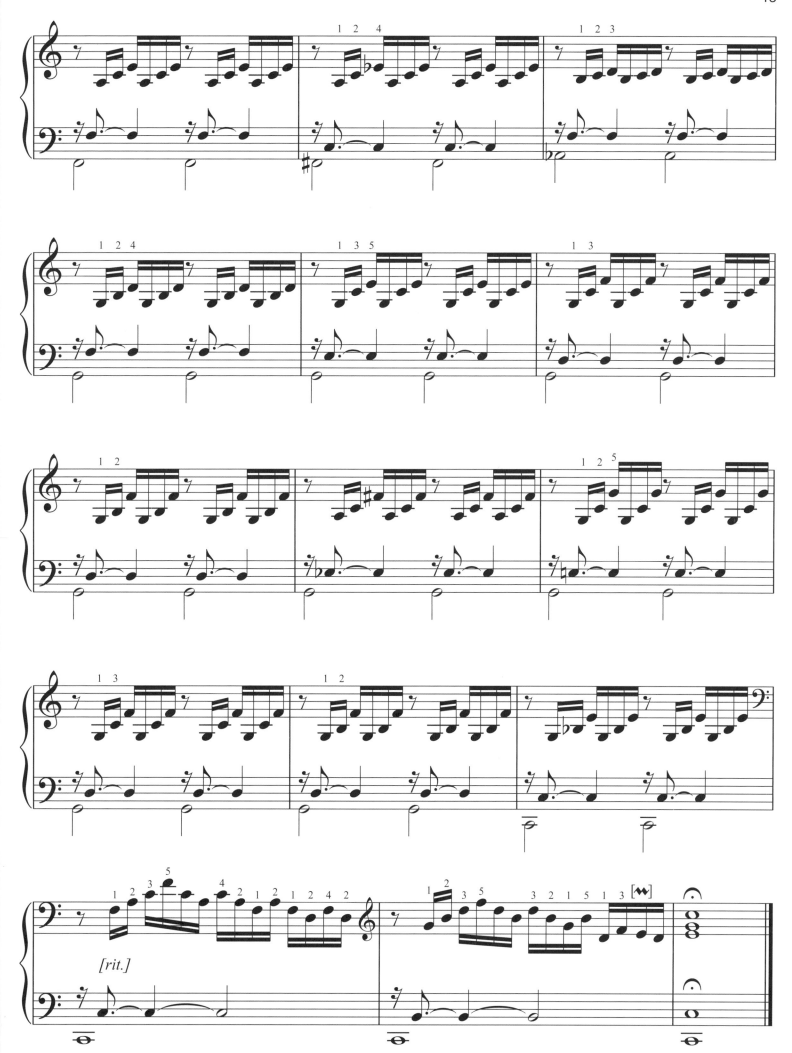

PRELUDE IN C MAJOR
BWV 939

JOHANN SEBASTIAN BACH
1685–1750

Moderato

SHORT AND LONG LEGATO
from *The First Term at the Piano*

BÉLA BARTÓK
1881–1945

Moderato ♩ = 52

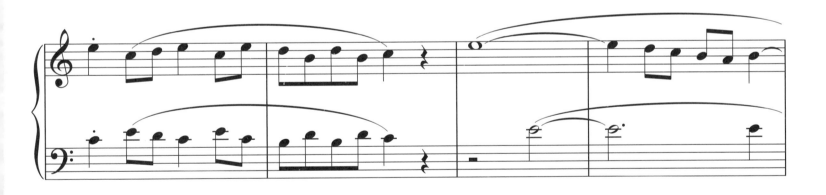

WALKING
from *The First Term at the Piano*

BÉLA BARTÓK
1881–1945

GERMAN DANCE IN C MAJOR

WoO 8, No. 1

LUDWIG VAN BEETHOVEN
1770–1827

LÄNDLER IN D MAJOR
WoO 11, No. 4

LUDWIG VAN BEETHOVEN
1770–1827

ECOSSAISE IN G MAJOR
WoO 23

LUDWIG VAN BEETHOVEN
1770–1827

Allegretto

ECOSSAISE IN E-FLAT MAJOR
WoO 86

LUDWIG VAN BEETHOVEN
1770–1827

ARIETTA IN C MAJOR

from *An Introduction to the Art of Playing on the Pianoforte*, Op. 42

MUZIO CLEMENTI
1752–1832

SPIRITOSO
from *Sonata in C Major*, Op. 36, No.1

MUZIO CLEMENTI
1752–1832

Spiritoso

COURANTE IN C MAJOR

JOHN BLOW
c. 1648–1708

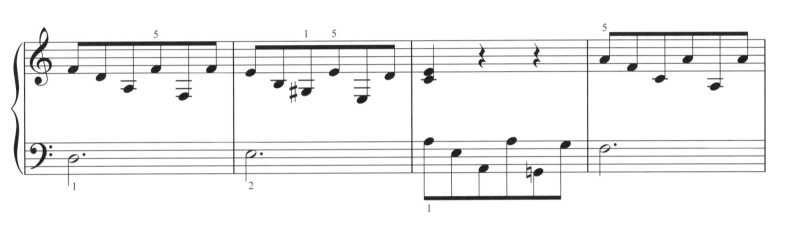

ARABESQUE
from *25 Progressive Studies*, Op. 100, No. 2

JOHANN FRIEDRICH BURGMÜLLER
1806–1874

Allegro scherzando (♩ = 152)

SONATINA IN C MAJOR

WILLIAM DUNCOMBE
c. 1736–c. 1818

THE CHASE

WILLIAM DUNCOMBE
c. 1736–c. 1818

Allegro [♩ = c. 80]

SPINNING SONG
Op. 14, No. 4

ALBERT ELLMENREICH
1816–1905

GAGLIARDA IN G MINOR

GIROLAMO FRESCOBALDI
1583–1643

Moderato

MORNING PRAYER

from *Albumleaves for the Young*, Op. 101, No. 2

CORNELIUS GURLITT
1820–1901

WALTZ IN C MAJOR

from *Albumleaves for the Young*, Op. 101, No. 11

CORNELIUS GURLITT
1820–1901

D.C. al Fine

TO SCHOOL
from *The First Lessons*, Op. 117, No. 14

CORNELIUS GURLITT
1820–1901

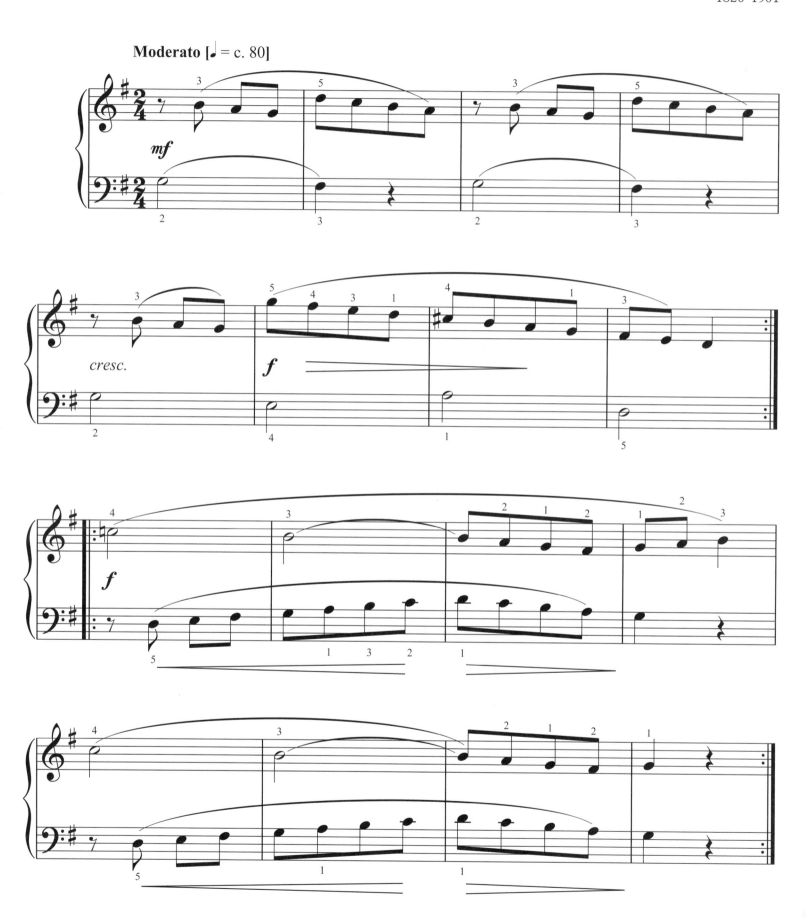

CRADLE SONG
from *The First Lessons*, Op. 117, No. 17

CORNELIUS GURLITT
1820–1901

IMPERTINENCE
(Bourrée)
HWV 494

GEORGE FRIDERIC HANDEL
1685–1759

MINUET IN F MAJOR

GEORGE FRIDERIC HANDEL
1685–1759

RIGAUDON IN G MAJOR

GEORGE FRIDERIC HANDEL
1685–1759

COUNTRY DANCE IN C MAJOR

FRANZ JOSEPH HAYDN
1732–1809

Allegretto

DANCE IN G MAJOR

FRANZ JOSEPH HAYDN
1732–1809

AIR IN A-FLAT MAJOR

K. Anh. 109b, Nr. 8 (15ff)

WOLFGANG AMADEUS MOZART
1756–1791

MINUET IN G MAJOR

K. 1e/1f

WOLFGANG AMADEUS MOZART
1756–1791

Fine

[poco rit. last time]

Trio

MINUET IN F MAJOR
K. 2

WOLFGANG AMADEUS MOZART
1756–1791

[Allegretto]

ALLEGRO IN B-FLAT MAJOR
K. 3

WOLFGANG AMADEUS MOZART
1756–1791

Allegro [♩ = ca. 120–126]

MINUET IN C MAJOR
K. 6

WOLFGANG AMADEUS MOZART
1756–1791

[Andante moderato]

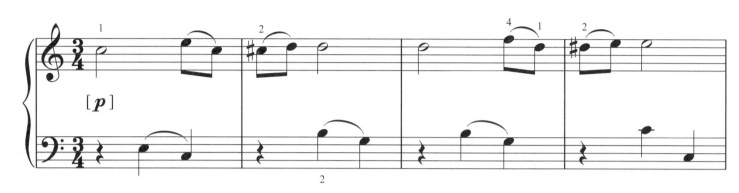

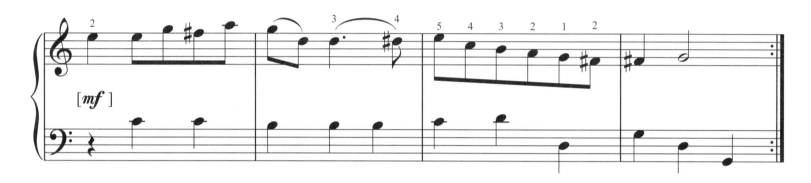

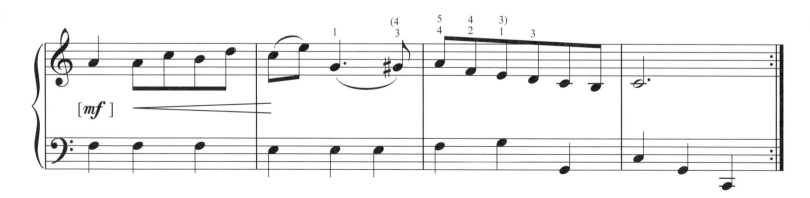

MENUET EN RONDEAU
(Minuet in the form of a Rondo)

JEAN-PHILIPPE RAMEAU
1683–1764

[Play quarter notes slightly detached throughout.]

MINUET IN G MAJOR
BWV Appendix 114

CHRISTIAN PETZOLD
1677–1733

Allegretto

MINUET IN G MINOR
BWV Appendix 115

CHRISTIAN PETZOLD
1677–1733

ARIA IN D MINOR

ALESSANDRO SCARLATTI
1660–1725

SONATA IN C MAJOR
L. 217 (K. 73b, P. 80)

DOMENICO SCARLATTI
1685–1757

[Allegro]

WALTZ IN A-FLAT MAJOR
Op. 9, No. 12 (D. 365)

FRANZ SCHUBERT
1797–1828

Allegretto e dolce

MELODY
from *Album for the Young*, Op. 68, No. 1

ROBERT SCHUMANN
1810–1856

SOLDIER'S MARCH
from *Album for the Young*, Op. 68, No. 2

ROBERT SCHUMANN
1810–1856

Allegro deciso (♩ = 132)

LITTLE PIECE
from *Album for the Young,* Op. 68, No. 5

ROBERT SCHUMANN
1810–1856

Nicht schnell
Not fast

THE DOLL'S BURIAL

from *Album for the Young*, Op. 39, No. 8

PYOTR IL'YICH TCHAIKOVSKY
1840–1893

RUSSIAN SONG

from *Album for the Young*, Op. 39, No. 11

PYOTR IL'YICH TCHAIKOVSKY
1840–1893

DANCE IN G MAJOR

GEORG PHILIPP TELEMANN
1681–1767

LITTLE RONDO IN F MAJOR

DANIEL GOTTLOB TÜRK
1750–1813

AMABILE
from Sonatina in C Major

CHARLES HENRY WILTON
1761–1832

Amabile

MINUET
from Sonatina in C Major

CHARLES HENRY WILTON
1761–1832